To:

_____

From:

_____

Date:

_____

Message:

_____

_____

_____

Bread from My Oven

Majorie Parker

MOODY
The Name You Can Trust®
A MINISTRY OF MOODY BIBLE INSTITUTE

BREAD FROM MY OVEN by Marjorie Parker

© 1999: Christian Art
PO Box 1599
Vereeniging
1930
South Africa

This book was first published in the United States by Moody Press with the title of *Bread from my Oven*, copyright © 1972 by the Moody Bible Institute of Chicago.

Designed by: Christian Art

ISBN 08024-4754-6

Printed in Singapore.

Bread upon the waters

*Cast your bread upon the waters, for after many days you
will find it again ... As you do not know the path of the
wind, or how the body is formed in a mother's womb, so
you cannot understand the work of God, the Maker of all
things. Sow your seed in the morning, and at evening let not
your hands be idle, for you do not know which will succeed,
whether this or that, or whether both will do equally well.*
Ecclesiastes 11:1-6

*I*f you are looking for a formula that will send forth the
members of the family to their daily tasks with cheerful
hearts prepared for discouragements, disappointments
or blighted hopes, then one may be found in the family
altar.

Father and Mother will be stronger for the work ahead
and determined to glorify God in whatever comes.

The family will be conscious throughout the day of
the presence of the Holy Spirit so that they may be "more

than conquerors" over all temptations that would ensnare them.

Home relationships and homelife will be sweetened. Misunderstandings will be resolved and frictions relieved, when the family prays together. Guests in the home will be blessed and friendships will be hallowed.

Best of all, it will be bread cast upon the waters which will give you 100 percent returns. Through family devotions, the eternal salvation of the children may be determined; and when the boys and girls have left the home, they will be held by the Christian ideal.

"Praying always with all prayer and supplication in the Spirit, and watching thereunto with all perseverance and supplication for all saints" (Eph 6:18).

A wise woman

The wise woman builds her house, but with her
own hands the foolish one tears hers down.
Proverbs 14:1

A good Christian home doesn't just happen. It is not the automatic result of seeing that the family is fed, clothed, and bathed daily. It is much more.

The wise woman (or the mother who cares) draws up some plans. She goes to the Bible daily for divine instruction in the building of her home. With Jesus Christ as the foundation, this house will stand against the storms of life.

"And, Thou, Lord, in the beginning hast laid the foundation of the earth; and the heavens are the works of thine hands" (Heb 1:10). Surely we can depend on the One who laid the foundation of the earth!

But this house must have walls – walls of prayer to keep Satan out, then "salvation will God appoint for

8

walls and bulwarks" (Isa 26:1).

"Except the Lord build the house, they labour in vain that build it" (Ps 127:1).

O God, our help in ages past,
Our hope for years to come,
Our shelter from the stormy blast,
And our eternal home.
~ Isaac Watts ~

House beautiful

*Do not store up for yourselves treasures on
earth, where moth and rust destroy, and where
thieves break in and steal. But store up for yourselves
treasures in heaven, where moth and rust do not destroy,
and where thieves do not break in and steal. For
where your treasure is, there your heart will be also.*
Matthew 6:19-21

*A*ll of us desire a lovely home with comfortable and
attractive furnishings. Certainly our Lord would have
us to be concerned with the comfort and welfare of the
families He has entrusted to us.

But it is so easy to think more highly of these things
than we ought to think. Our sense of values becomes
somewhat upset when we put too great a value on things
material.

Oliver Wendell Holmes said, "We sometimes mortgage
a house for the mahogany we bring into it. Beauty is a

great thing, but beauty of garment, house, and furniture are tawdry ornaments compared with domestic love. All the elegance in the world will not make a home, and I would give more for a spoonful of real hearty love than for whole shiploads of furniture and all the gorgeousness the world can gather."

What does God's Word say?

"Better is little with the fear of the Lord than great treasure and trouble therewith" (Pr 15:16-17).

"It is better to dwell in a corner of the housetop, than with a brawling woman in a wide house" (Pr 21:9).

O think of the home over there,
By the side of the river of light,
Where the saints all immortal and fair
Are robed in their garments of white.
~ D.W.C. Huntington ~

To love and to cherish

*Dear friends, let us love one another, for love comes
from God. Everyone who loves has been born
of God and knows God. Whoever does not love does
not know God, because God is love. This is how God
showed his love among us: He sent his one and only Son
into the world that we might live through him. This is love:
not that we loved God, but that he loved us and sent his
Son as an atoning sacrifice for our sins. Dear friends,
since God so loved us, we also ought to love one another.
1 John 4:7-12*

"A feeling of strong personal attachment induced by
sympathetic understanding" is the way Webster defines
love. But we know love as that tender, considerate
affection that we all need. It is the greatest of these three:
faith, hope, and love.

Christians should walk in love. We should love God
supremely, and our neighbor as ourselves. One indication

12

that we have eternal life is that we love God and the brethren, for he that loves, has God and knows God.

Does your heart ever feel bereft of love? Benjamin Franklin said, "If you wish to be loved, be lovable."

Remember that love is a fruit of the Spirit and that love must be shed abroad in our hearts by the Holy Spirit. So if you want more love, you must be filled with the Spirit. If you are filled with God's love, you will become a channel and God will love others through your love.

"Be kindly affectioned one to another with brotherly love; in honor preferring one another" (Ro 12:10).

Love lifted me! Love lifted me!
When nothing else could help,
Love lifted me.
~ James Rowe ~

The tongue

*Do not let any unwholesome talk come out of your mouths,
but only what is helpful for building others up according to
their needs, that it may benefit those who listen. And do not
grieve the Holy Spirit of God, with whom you were sealed
for the day of redemption. Get rid of all bitterness, rage and
anger, brawling and slander, along with every form of
malice. Be kind and compassionate to one another,
forgiving each other, just as in Christ God forgave you.*
Ephesians 4:29-32

Enjoyment and relaxation can come to the housewife
by a friendly chat with a neighbor over a cup of coffee
after the children have been hustled off to school. Or a
pleasant conversation over the telephone can brighten
one's day. On the other hand, much harm can be done to
another's life and reputation if such an innocent pastime
as mentioned here is turned into a gossip session.

The Bible deals more severely with the tongue than

with any other member of the human body. For one person "corrupt communication" may be profanity; for another it may be subtle innuendo, and for another, gossip.

What can be done? Refrain from any speech except that which will edify or build up the hearers in the knowledge of whatsoever things are true, honest, just, pure, lovely, and of good report.

Napoleon said that we rule men with words. How carefully, then, these words ought to be chosen and weighed before being uttered.

"Let the words of my mouth, and the meditation of my heart, be acceptable in thy sight, O Lord, my strength, and my redeemer" (Ps 19:14).

O for a thousand tongues to sing
My great Redeemer's praise,
The glories of my God and King,
The triumphs of His grace.
~ Charles Wesley ~

"No thanks"

Praise the Lord, O my soul; all my inmost being, praise his
holy name. Praise the Lord, O my soul, and forget not all
his benefits – who forgives all your sins and heals all your
diseases, who redeems your life from the pit and crowns
you with love and compassion ...
Psalm 103:1-7

Isn't it strange that very often we forget to thank God
for our blessings until it suddenly dawns on us that
Thanksgiving Day is here, and that it is a day when we
are supposed to give thanks for all of life's bounties.

Too often the real purpose of the day is obscured by
the frenzy of getting the groceries in, the turkey cooked,
the dressing made, the table set, the house cleaned, et
cetera, ad infinitum!

A real comprehension of the truths which cluster about
Thanksgiving can come only by a service of praise at
church, or a quiet time spent alone with God and His

word.

It seems so much easier to be conscious of problems and cares which are about to overwhelm us, than it is to "Count your many blessings, name them one by one, and it will surprise you what the Lord has done."

But when we take inventory of all our blessings our problems and burdens seem to fade into insignificance.

"Giving thanks always for all things unto God and the Father in the name of our Lord Jesus Christ" (Eph 5:20).

When morning gilds the skies,
My heart awaking cries,
May Jesus Christ be praised:
Alike at work and prayer,
To Jesus I repair;
May Jesus Christ be praised.
~Trans. from the German by
Edward Caswell ~

Not by bread alone

Be careful to follow every command I am giving you to-day
... Remember how the Lord your God led you all the way in
the desert these forty years, to humble you and to test you
in order to know what was in your heart ...
Deuteronomy 8:1-3

$\mathcal{H}$ippies today use the word bread to mean money, or cash. This would indicate that even in their thinking, bread is necessary to life, just as is the coin of the realm.

But the Word of God tells us that man does not live by bread alone – be it food *or* cash – but by "every word that proceedeth out of the mouth of the Lord."

It would follow then that man (or woman) would do well to take heed of "every word that proceedeth out of the mouth of the Lord."

Where may we find such words? Where can we go to find guidance for our daily walk? "Thy word have I hid in mine heart, that I might not sin against thee"

(Ps 119:11).

There are many things that money (or "bread") *can* buy. But they are not the things that make for happiness. Money can help to make us more comfortable in this world – comfortable in our misery sometimes – but food for the soul comes from the Word of God and communion with Him. Feed on His Word. The nourishment is there for the taking.

> *Ere you left your room this morning*
> *Did you think to pray?*
> *In the name of Christ, our Saviour,*
> *Did you sue for loving favor,*
> *As a shield today?*
> *~ Mrs. M.A. Kidder ~*

Speaker of the house

Wives, submit to your husbands as to the Lord ...
Husbands, love your wives, just as Christ loved the
church and gave himself up for her to make her holy
... He who loves his wife loves himself ... However,
each one of you also must love his wife as he loves
himself, and the wife must respect her husband.
Ephesians 5:22-33

*T*here are many times and situations when the wife
and mother is obliged to be the "speaker of the house."

Those mothers whose homes are broken, or whose
husbands are in the service of their country, of necessity
must act as head of the house.

In normal circumstances, however, this is not God's
way. He does things decently and in order and anything
with two heads is a monstrosity. So there must be only
one head in every home. This is clearly stated in His
Word, "For the husband is the head of the wife" (v. 23).

The wife who is submissive to her husband in love makes it easy for him to obey the scriptural injunction, "So ought men to love their wives as their own bodies" (v. 28).

Someone has said, "Some women cling to their own houses like the honeysuckle over the door, yet, like it, sweeten all the region with the subtle fragrance of their goodness."

Saviour, teach me day by day,
Love's sweet lesson to obey;
Sweeter lesson cannot be,
Loving Him who first loved me.
~ Jane E. Leeson ~

Blessing in disguise

But I tell you: Love your enemies and pray
for those who persecute you, that you may be
sons of your Father in heaven ... Be perfect,
therefore, as your heavenly Father is perfect.
Matthew 5:44-48

Two nurses came to a doctor saying they could not bear serving a certain patient who was most trying. The doctor pointed out to them that the patient was educating them, and such training was well worth paying for. He told them that if they could stand it they would reap the benefit throughout life; they would be tempered and nothing would be too hard for them again. They took up the work once more from a different point of view and never complained again.

In our humanity it is difficult to understand sometimes, but it is well to remember in times of trial that there is a bright side to all things and a good God over all.

Charles Haddon Spurgeon said, "Somewhere or other in the worst flood of trouble there always is a dry spot for contentment to get its foot on, and if there were not it would learn to swim."

"And we know that all things work together for good to them that love God, to them who are the called according to his purpose" (Ro 8:28).

Just when I need Him, Jesus is near,
Just when I falter, just when I fear;
Ready to help me, ready to cheer,
Just when I need Him most.
~ William C. Poole ~

Joy bells

*Be careful not to do your "acts of righteousness"
before men, to be seen by them. If you do, you will
have no reward from your Father in heaven ... But
when you give to the needy, do not let your left
hand know what your right hand is doing, so that
your giving may be in secret. Then your Father,
who sees what is done in secret, will reward you.*
Matthew 6:1-4

Are you one of those rare people who can do a friend
a favor on the sly? Or do you have to "sound a trumpet"
when you do a good deed, so that all the world may
know?

There is a special kind of satisfaction that comes from
doing good and keeping it a secret. Those who practice
this higher altruism know an inner joy experienced by
very few indeed.

This type of Christian service will ring joy bells that

24

have never been heard before, bringing joy to the recipient of the deed as well as joy to the doer.

Of course the secret joy spreader must cultivate this trait. It will not come naturally, because it goes against the grain of our ego. We want others to recognize any noble or unselfish act of ours.

Jesus was our wonderful example of doing good secretly. He warned against ostentatious charity and admonished His followers, "Take heed that ye do not your alms before men, to be seen of them" (Mt 6:1).

When He healed the leper He told him, "See that thou tell no man," and left the scene at once.

Ring the bells of heaven! there is joy today,
For a soul returning from the wild!
See! the Father meets him out upon the way,
Welcoming His weary, wand'ring child.
~ William O. Cushing ~

Tell him you love him

If anyone acknowledges that Jesus is the Son of God, God lives in him and he in God ... If anyone says, "I love God," yet hates his brother, he is a liar. For anyone who does not love his brother, whom he has seen, cannot love God, whom he has not seen. And he has given us this command: Whoever loves God must also love his brother.
1 John 4:15-21

*E*very wife knows that to speak the simple sentence, "I love you," will ease strained relations and restore fellowship in many domestic situations. Any husband is pleased to have his wife repeat these three little magic words.

Often a child's attitude can be changed from stubborn rebellion to submissive obedience by Mother's simply saying to him, "I love you," accompanied of course by a smile which tells him she really means it.

Who is not made happier by a sincere verbal

expression of love?

So also, the loving heart of our God must be warmed when we tell Him that we love Him. He above all, through Christ Jesus, is worthy of the frequent expression of our love.

One look at a sunrise should cause us to exclaim, "I love thee, my Jesus."

One note of birdsong should prompt us to sing out, "I love thee, my Lord."

The heart's view of Calvary should inspire us to respond,

My Jesus, I love Thee,
I know Thou art mine;
For Thee all the follies of sin I resign;
My gracious Redeemer, my Saviour art Thou;
If ever I loved Thee, my Jesus, 'tis now.
~ W.R. Featherstone ~

Words of wisdom

*Listen, my son, accept what I say, and the years
of your life will be many. I guide you in the way of
wisdom and lead you along straight paths. When you
walk, your steps will not be hampered; when you
run, you will not stumble. Hold on to instruction,
do not let it go; guard it well, for it is your life.*
Proverbs 4:10-13

*T*hese strong words are appropriate for young sons
and older sons, as well as daughters young and old.

All who are in Christ through faith in Him are the
possessors of an all-sufficient Saviour, and have come
to a knowledge which far exceeds all the knowledge
and wisdom of the world, with all its progress in the arts
and sciences.

To believe on Christ who is Wisdom from God is to
possess real life, true liberty. Christ is wisdom indeed.

There are enough stumbling blocks and pitfalls in the

28

paths of young people today. Surely they need all the help they can get so that when they run they will not stumble.

Blessed is the youngster – or teenager – who will "take fast hold of instruction; let her not go: keep her; for she is thy life" (v. 13).

God's instruction book will tell us the way if we will study it; for He says, "I am the way, the truth, and the life: no man cometh unto the Father, but by me" (Jn 14:6).

Saviour, teach me day by day,
Love's sweet lesson to obey;
Sweeter lesson cannot be,
Loving Him who first loved me.
~ Jane E. Leeson ~

The bread of idleness

A wife of noble character who can find? ... she provides food for her family ... She watches over the affairs of her household and does not eat the bread of idleness ...
Proverbs 31:10-31

M any housewives today are complaining about being bored to death. Our government and others are spending billions of dollars to provide entertainment for our leisure hours. Labor unions are striking with demands for shorter workweeks and more leisure time for workers.

Why is it that some busy wives and mothers never find enough hours in the day to do the many tasks at hand, while others seem oblivious to their duties and spend the daytime hours chatting on the telephone or sipping a cup of coffee at the neighbor's?

Surely there is no harm, and sometimes much to be gained, by a friendly visit with a neighbor. But as in all things, the concerned housewife and mother will not allow these pleasantries to take too large a share of her time lest she be guilty of eating "the bread of idleness."

It is no secret that work has a therapeutic value and that one is happiest when busy. Working in the sunshine among the flowers has helped to heal many a broken heart.

Any woman who "looks well to the ways of her household" will have no time to become bored. Instead, "Strength and honour are her clothing; and she shall rejoice in time to come" (v. 25).

The sweetest lives are those to duty wed,
Whose deeds, both great and small,
Are close-knit strands of unbroken thread
Where love ennobles all.
The world may sound no trumpets, ring no bells;
The book of life the shining record tells.

Attributed to
~ Elizabeth Barrett Browning ~

Senior citizens

*A man's steps are directed by the Lord. How then
can anyone understand his own way? ... The lamp of
the Lord searches the spirit of a man; it searches out
his inmost being. Love and faithfulness keep a king
safe; through love his throne is made secure ...*
Proverbs 20:24-29

There comes a time for all of us when we must face
the fact that the years are piling up and we are no longer
young. The telltale wrinkles are a little deeper than the
last time we looked.

So what? Someone has said, "If wrinkles must be
written upon your brow, let them not be written upon
the heart. The spirit should not grow old."

Old age is blessed if you let it come naturally. You
cannot hide it. Oh, you may cover the wrinkles for a
while, but not for long. If the time has come for you to
be old do not be ashamed of it!

Did you ever stop to think that the grandest things in the universe are old – mountains, rivers, seas, stars, even eternity. Old age is glorious if found in the way of righteousness.

In describing the aged man, Solomon likens the whiteness of his locks to the blossoming of the almond tree. "A hoary head is a crown of glory." When one comes to the end of the path of life, there may be no color in the cheek, no luster in the eye, no spring in the step, yet around the head of the aged one who has been "faithful unto death" there may glow a glory brighter than ever bloomed in an almond tree.

My latest sun is sinking fast,
My race is nearly run;
My strongest trials now are past
My triumph is begun.
~ J. Hascall ~

What'll I wear?

Who of you by worrying can add a single hour to his life?
And why do you worry about clothes? See how the lilies of
the field grow. They do not labor or spin. Yet I tell you that
not even Solomon in all his splendor was dressed like one
of these. If that is how God clothes the grass of the field,
which is here today and tomorrow is thrown into the fire,
will he not much more clothe you, O you of little faith?
Matthew 6:27-30

This is a dilemma faced by the average woman almost every day. And a question the average husband probably is tired of hearing. There can be a closet full of clothes, yet there doesn't seem to be just the right dress for the occasion!

"Clothes make the man" it is said, and some might argue with this, but at least clothes make the woman feel more comfortable. And she is more at ease when she knows she is appropriately dressed.

There is much we can learn from the flowers which wear such beautiful garments. "And why take ye thought for raiment? Consider the lilies of the field, how they grow; they toil not, neither do they spin: and yet I say unto you, That even Solomon in all his glory was not arrayed like one of these" (vs. 28,29).

Flowers do not save their best clothes for Sunday, but wear their lovely raiment and give forth their perfume every day. So let our Christian lives, free from stain, give forth the fragrance of the love of God.

O Jesus, I have promised
To serve Thee to the end;
Be Thou forever near me,
My Master and my Friend;
I shall not fear the battle
If Thou art by my side,
Nor wander from the pathway
If Thou wilt be my Guide.
~ John E. Bode ~

Stars

*Those who are wise will shine like the bright-
ness of the heavens, and those who lead many
to righteousness, like the stars for ever and ever.*
Daniel 12:3

Outer space has come in for a great deal of attention
in our modern day. The sun and moon and stars are being
rediscovered and we are looking at them as though seeing
them for the first time.

The Bible has much to say about the stars. God knows
how many there are, and He has given each one a name
(Ps 147:4). And it was a particularly bright star that led
the Magi on the road to Jerusalem two thousand years
ago.

Modern day astronomers with their technological
advances, their powerful telescopes and computers, have
added much to our knowledge of these heavenly bodies.
But no one has yet been able to count the stars! "Look

now toward heaven, and tell the stars, if thou be able to number them" (Gen 15:5).

It may be that God gave us the stars in their beauty to cause us to look up – up and away from ourselves and our daily frustrations and fears to take a far look away from ourselves. Better still, let us look beyond the stars to God who made them!

"Is not God in the height of heaven? and behold the height of the stars, how high they are" (Job 22:12).

I am thinking today of that beautiful land
I shall reach when the sun goeth down;
when thro' wonderful grace
by my Saviour I stand,
Will there be any stars in my crown?
~ Eliza E. Hewitt ~

"Thank You"

*Let them give thanks to the Lord for his unfailing
love and his wonderful deeds for men, for he satisfies
the thirsty and fills the hungry with good things ...
Psalm 107:8,9*

A mature Christian is one who can say "Thank You" to God when her husband fails to get that long-hoped-for raise in salary; or Johnnie brings home an "F" on his report card; or the baby comes down with measles in spite of all precautions.

When troubles pile up around us we can easily forget that He knows the end from the beginning and that this thing is going to work out for our good, no matter how dark the picture looks at the present time.

We forget that one must suffer before he can be healed.

If our gratitude depends on outward circumstances, it does not occupy a permanent place in our lives. When the winds of adversity blow, and we are in trouble and need help and still can say to God "Thank You," we have gained spiritually.

Are you lonely? Are you hungry? "He satisfieth the longing soul, and filleth the hungry soul with goodness" (v. 9).

Have you ever said "Thank You" to God for the warmth of the sun, the fragrance of a flower, the love of a child?

Thank you, Lord, for saving my soul.
Thank you, Lord for making me whole.
Thank you, Lord, for giving to me
Thy great salvation so rich and free.
~ Seth Sykes ~

Worry wart

In that day this song will be sung in the land of Judah: We have a strong city; God makes salvation its walls and ramparts ... Trust in the Lord forever, for the Lord, the Lord, is the Rock eternal.
Isaiah 26:1-4

Worry! Fret! Stew! Satan is pleased when that is the order of the day for us.

Faith and worry cannot be reconciled. Worry is a great hindrance to spiritual progress. God does not will that His own should be irritable, embittered, robbed of sleep, and have the peace of home destroyed by worry.

All the promises in His Word are given as insurance against such. No child of God who believes sincerely that all things work together for his good could constantly worry.

The first time you evaluate a situation and realize that it is beyond you, commit it to God and stop worrying.

Satan would have you turn your mind into a merry-go-round. He is the instigator of worry which displeases our Lord.

If we are children of God, let us quit this bad business of worrying. Why worry when you can pray?

"Peace I leave with you, my peace I give unto you: not as the world giveth, give I unto you. Let not your heart be troubled, neither let it be afraid" (Jn 14:27).

Have we trials and temptations?
Is there trouble anywhere?
We should never be discouraged,
Take it to the Lord in prayer.
~ Joseph Scriven ~

The bread of God

*So they asked him, "What miraculous sign then will you
give that we may see it and believe you? ..." Jesus said to
them, "I tell you the truth, it is not Moses who has given
you the bread from heaven, but it is my Father who gives
you the true bread from heaven ..." "Sir," they said, "from
now on give us this bread." Then Jesus declared, "I am the
bread of life. He who comes to me will never go hungry,
and he who believes in me will never be thirsty."*
John 6:30-35

Jesus is indeed the Bread of Life. He is the bread of
God. Bread is a term used for food in a general sense.

Bread is essential as food for the body. Just so, there
can be no spiritual life without Jesus.

Bread satisfies hunger, and every soul without Christ
is a hungry soul. Oh, poor hungry soul, come to Jesus!
He is the Bread that satisfies.

Bread is good to the taste. Nearly everyone thinks that

his mother's bread was the best ever baked. There is no odor so pleasing to the olfactory sense as that of bread baking. Even now, in memory we can smell the delicious scent being wafted through the house. This is one of the most pleasant memories of childhood.

Bread gives strength. Weak soul, feed upon Jesus. He will strengthen you. "I can do all things through Christ which strengtheneth me" (Phil 4:13).

Surely the "bread" that God provides is good. "Oh taste and see that the Lord is good."

My hope is built on nothing less
Than Jesus' blood and righteousness;
I dare not trust the sweetest frame,
But wholly lean on Jesus' name.
~ Edward Mote ~

Patience

... The seed is the word of God, Those along the path are the ones who hear ... the devil comes and takes away the word ... so they may not believe and be saved. Those on the rock ... believe for a while, but in the time of testing they fall away. The seed that fell among thorns stands for those who hear, but ... they do not mature. But the seed on good soil stands for those with a noble and good heart, who hear the word, retain it, and by persevering produce a crop.
Luke 8:4-15

One commodity that busy mothers are short on is patience. Just when you feel you have all your ducks in a row calamity strikes the household and patience flies out the window.

All of us praise patience, but few practice it. When the bones are aching with weariness; when time is running out and there is much yet to be done, Mom can lose patience and become irritable and cross.

But "natural" feelings must not rule the Christian, or what is her Christianity worth?

Remembering our patient Saviour ought to make it easier for His children to be patient.

"Grin and bear it is the old fashioned advice, but sing and bear it is a great deal better." So said Charles Haddon Spurgeon.

"What can't be cured must be endured," is true.

When our hearts are right with God how wonderfully He gives much grace to bear even the heaviest yoke. Only those with God's love in their hearts can sing at labor while others murmur.

Sing the wondrous love of Jesus,
Sing His mercy and His grace;
In the mansions bright and blessed,
He'll prepare for us a place.
~ Eliza E. Hewitt ~

What's in a name?

*She will give birth to a son, and you are to give him
the name Jesus, because he will save his people
from their sins. All this took place to fulfil what the
Lord had said through the prophet: "The virgin will be
with child and will give birth to a son, and they will
call him Immanuel" – which means, "God with us."*
Matthew 1:21-23

*L*oving parents very carefully select just the right name
for that precious, newborn baby. Many children are
named for relatives who are dear to the parents. At any
rate, much thought is usually given to the naming of a
child.

Some of the men in Scripture were named by God to
indicate their characters or a blessing from God. This is
why Jacob had his name changed to Israel and why
Simon had his name changed to Peter.

Likewise, the names of Christ show His person and

work. They reveal what He is and what He came to do. All of them are significant, for they all have important meaning for us; they unveil His true character.

The name "Jesus" was given by the angel to Joseph before Christ was born. It literally means "Saviour." Christ came to save us from our sins and to give us fellowship with God Himself.

The name Emmanuel, which means, "God with us," emphasizes the constant presence of God.

"A good name is rather to be chosen than great riches, and loving favour rather than silver and gold" (Pr 22:1).

Take the name of Jesus with you,
Child of sorrow and of woe;
It will joy and comfort give you,
Take it, then, where'er you go.
~ Mrs. Lydia Baxter ~

New year's resolutions

*For Christ's love compels us, because we are convinced
that one died for all, and therefore all died. And he died for
all, that those who live should no longer live for themselves
but for him who died for them and was raised again ...*
2 Corinthians 5:14-17

Resolutions may be made and broken year after year,
but it never hurt anyone to keep on making them. Better
to live up to them for even a little while than never make
them at all! And stifling a good impulse is never wise.

Of course resolutions made in the energy of the flesh,
and resolutions dependent on one's own strength for their
fulfillment, are easily forgotten, broken, or neglected.

But it is a different story when one determines by the
help of the Lord to strengthen a weak place, or spread a
little more joy in a sad world, or show a lost one the
way of salvation.

Every New Year holds golden opportunities which we

48

often let slip through our hands. When the strength of the Lord is relied upon, definite progress in the spiritual life will be made.

Never hesitate to follow your good impulses in making resolutions, then trust God for the power to carry them out!

Father, Thy mercies past we own,
Thy still continued care;
To Thee presenting, through Thy Son,
Whate'er we have or are.
Our residue of days or hours
Thine, wholly Thine, shall be;
And all our consecrated powers
A sacrifice to Thee.
~ Charles Wesley ~

Rejoice evermore!

*Though the fig tree does not bud and there are no
grapes on the vines, though the olive crop fails and
the fields produce no food, though there are no sheep
in the pen and no cattle in the stalls, yet I will rejoice
in the Lord, I will be joyful in God my Savior ...*
Habakkuk 3:17-19

*N*o one but a Christian can be truly happy and every
Christian ought to be supremely happy. We do not have
to wait until we get to heaven to be happy. Our eternal
life begins as soon as we let Jesus come into our hearts.

This is not the type of joy which kicks up its heels or
laughs raucously, but rather the deep-seated peace which
comes from the knowledge that sins have been forgiven
and "your body is the temple of the Holy Ghost which
is in you, which ye have of God, and ye are not your
own" (1 Co 6:19).

This is a joy that is permanent and is not tied to

circumstances.

The Christian will be "found unto praise and honour and glory at the appearing of Jesus Christ"; but Peter adds, "Whom having not seen, ye love; in whom, though now ye see Him not, yet believing, ye rejoice with joy unspeakable and full of glory" (1 Pe 1:7,8).

This is a joy that comes as a by-product of the acceptance of God's great gift – the Lord Jesus Christ.

"Glory ye in his holy name: let the heart of them rejoice that seek the Lord" (1 Ch 16:10).

Come, we that love the Lord,
And let our joys be known;
Join in a song with sweet accord,
And thus surround the throne.
~ Isaac Watts ~

Work and worship

*From heaven the Lord looks down and sees
all mankind; from his dwelling place he
watches all who live on earth– he who forms the
hearts of all, who considers everything they do.*
Psalm 33:13-15

No one can ever earn his salvation. "For by grace are ye saved through faith; and that not of yourselves: it is the gift of God: Not of works, lest any man should boast" (Eph 2:8-9).

After one has received this wonderful gift, however, his desire should be to serve the Saviour. "For they that are after the flesh do mind the things of the flesh; but they that are after the Spirit the things of the Spirit" (Ro 8:5).

Work, worship, and instruction are always the ingredients of Christian living. True worship of Christ always leads to the place of need where work should be

52

done. Then the busy Christian will constantly need to go to the Lord and His Word for instruction and admonition.

It does not matter where your work is, or whether it is visible. You may never see the results of your labor. Your name may never be associated with it. But you are working with eternity in view!

Make use of me, my God!
Let me not be forgot;
A broken vessel cast aside,
One whom Thou needest not.
All things do serve Thee here,
All creatures, great and small;
Make use of me, of me, my God –
The meanest of them all.
~ Horatius Bonar ~

The bread of tears

... Restore us, O God; make your face shine upon us, that we may be saved. O Lord God Almighty, how long will your anger smolder against the prayers of your people? You have fed them with the bread of tears; you have made them drink tears by the bowlful.
Psalm 80:1-5

Never be ashamed of your tears. Maudlin, cry-baby sobs are unbecoming in an adult, but tears of compassion or sympathy reveal qualities of the soul that this old world greatly needs.

Eight times Joseph is said to have wept; David seven times; and Jeremiah, the weeping prophet, three times. The shortest verse in the Bible tells us that "Jesus wept" (Jn 11:35).

God sends occasions to all when the greatest and the best of us give way to "the bread of tears."

God does not despise our tears. David pleaded, "Put

thou my tears into thy bottle; are they not in thy book?"
(Ps 56:8).

So to weep is not wrong, that is, if we weep over the right things.

There is the comforting promise in Isaiah 25:8, "He will swallow up death in victory, and the Lord God will wipe away tears from off all faces, and the rebuke of his people shall he take away from off all the earth: for the Lord hath spoken it."

God shall " wipe away all tears;"
There's no death, no pain, nor fears;
And they count not time by years,
For there is "no night there."
~ John R. Clements ~

Doers of the Word

Therefore, get rid of all moral filth and the evil that is so prevalent and humbly accept the word planted in you, which can save you. Do not merely listen to the word, and so deceive yourselves. Do what it says ...
James 1:21-25

To hear is easier than to do. We hear the Word of God over and over and even rejoice in it, yet fail to let it take hold in our lives so that we act upon it.

If we are to be doers of the Word we must act out its principles in our daily living.

This involves many things: "bringing into captivity every thought to the obedience of Christ" (2 Co 10:5), walking "in wisdom toward them that are without, redeeming the time" (Col 4:5), and showing "forth the praises of Him who hath called you out of darkness into His marvelous light" (1 Pe 2:9).

In other words we must try to live moment by moment

in the light of God's Word, "doing" according to the light it sheds upon our path.

We are clearly told that if we hear God's Word and do it not, we are deceiving ourselves.

One can look at his face in a mirror and quickly forget how he looked. So it is possible to see our spiritual image in the Word of God and forget how we appear.

God put His truths in His Book for our good. "Therefore we ought to give the more earnest heed to the things which we have heard, lest at any time we should let them slip" (Heb 2:1).

Queen for a day

Get wisdom, get understanding; do not forget my words or swerve from them. Do not forsake wisdom, and she will protect you ... Wisdom is supreme; therefore get wisdom. Though it cost all you have, get understanding ...
Proverbs 4:5-9

What fun it is to be granted a reprieve from housework for about twenty-four hours on your birthday or anniversary. The reprieve may take the form of breakfast in bed or dinner at a swank restaurant, and such luxurious treatment can produce a certain inner glow that will last for many days.

We read of a number of queens in the Bible. One was the famed Queen of Sheba who "came to Jerusalem with a very great train" to see with her own eyes if the stories of the splendor and majesty of Solomo's court were true. Convinced, before returning to her own country she said to Solomon, "The half was not told me: thy wisdom and prosperity exceedeth the fame which I heard" (1 Ki 10:7).

"Queen for a day" is about as long a reign as many of us will have here on earth. But what hope we have for the future! "If we suffer, we shall also reign with him" (2 Ti 2:12).

"The kingdoms of this world are become the kingdoms of our Lord, and of his Christ; and he shall reign for ever and ever" (Rev 11:15b).

Jesus shall reign where'er the sun
Does his successive journeys run;
His kingdom spread from shore to shore,
Till moons shall wax and wane no more.
~ Isaac Watts ~

From rags to riches

But just as you excel in everything – in faith, in speech, in knowledge, in complete earnestness and in your love for us – see that you also excel in this grace of giving ... For you know the grace of our Lord Jesus Christ, that though he was rich, yet for your sakes he became poor, so that you through his poverty might become rich.
2 Corinthians 8:7-9

$\mathcal{M}$any stories have been told about some famous person who rose from rags to riches. We have thrilled to learn how a life begun in poverty triumphed by hard work and diligence and attained great wealth.

We would be more surprised, however, if we read of one of great wealth who gave up his riches to those who were poor and less fortunate and by so doing became poor himself.

Not many stories have been told of any who have gone from riches to rags in order that others might become rich. Yet that is exactly what our Lord did. He came from the glories of heaven, where all that the Father possessed He possessed, to live His earthly life in poverty. His poverty was voluntary. He *chose* to do this for your sake and my sake.

"The foxes have holes and the birds of the air have nests; but the Son of Man hath not where to lay His head" (Mt 8:20).

What was it that made Him do this for you and for me? "That ye through His poverty might be rich" (v. 9).

Down from His glory, ever living story,
My God and Saviour came,
and Jesus was His name.
Born in a manger, To His own a stranger,
A man of sorrows, tears and agony.
~ William E. Booth-Clibborn ~

Let's demonstrate!

*Then they brought him a demon-possessed man who
was blind and mute, and Jesus healed him, so that he
could both talk and see ... But if I drive out demons
by the Spirit of God, then the kingdom of God has
come upon you ... He who is not with me is against
me, and he who does not gather with me scatters.*
Matthew 12:22-30

There are so many issues before us today that we are
compelled to take a stand on one side or the other. All
classes and types of people are carrying signs. We have
protesters, demonstrators, marchers, and rioters.

Ours is a world of challenge, change, and conflict.
Much time and money is spent in these interests today.

There is one issue we cannot dodge but must face
squarely. We cannot be neutral: What will you do with
Jesus?

If we do not line up on His side we are automatically

against Him. Jesus said, "He that is not with me is against me" (v. 30). If you don't want to be *against* Him then you must march *for* Him.

Let's demonstrate! Let's show the world what Christ can do with a life wholly committed to Him. He can bring real meaning and direction into the life of one completely dedicated to Him.

> *Take my life, and let it be*
> *Consecrated, Lord, to Thee;*
> *Take my hands, and let them move*
> *At the impulse of Thy love.*
> *~ Frances R. Havergal ~*

A morsel of bread

*"Let me get you something to eat, so you can be refreshed
and then go on your way – now that you have come to your
servant." "Very well," they answered, "do as you say."*
Genesis 18:5

*On the fourth day they got up early and he prepared to
leave, but the girl's father said to his son-in-law, "Refresh
yourself with something to eat; then you can go."*
Judges 19:5

*Now please listen to your servant and
let me give you some food so you may eat
and have the strength to go on your way.*
1 Samuel 28:22

We have many hungry people in the world today, and
we Christian people should do all in our power to see
that they are fed.

God does not intend for us to encourage laziness and

indolence, and many times our efforts to help others who could help themselves result in this; however, God does expect us to help those who are less fortunate than we. We should count it a privilege to share our "morsel of bread," and thank God we have some to share. "It is more blessed to give than to receive."

To feel the pangs of hunger and have no bread is tragic. Even more tragic are "they which do hunger and thirst after righteousness" and cannot find spiritual food.

The privilege and responsibility of the believer is to share his spiritual "morsel of bread" with a neighbor or friend, who may not have the opportunity of hearing the Word of God proclaimed by a godly pastor who is interested in winning the lost.

Is your life a channel of blessing?
Is it daily telling for Him?
Have you spoken the word of salvation
To those who are dying in sin?
~ H.G. Smyth ~

Do your own thing!

See, I am doing a new thing! Now it springs up; do you not perceive it? I am making a way in the desert and streams in the wasteland ...
Isaiah 43:19-21

$\mathcal{M}$uch talk has gone around lately among the so-called flower children about doing your own thing.

What is your particular "thing"? For the mother in the home it means being "all things to all men" for she is the hub of the wheel which keeps the home running.

The wife and mother cannot know what each day will hold for her and the loved ones in her household.

There will be new experiences, new challenges, new opportunities. There will be lessons to be learned, and undoubtedly new sorrows and heartaches.

But what is God's promise? "I will do a new thing" – more than we could ask or think. What do we want from God for our personal lives?

A greater knowledge of His Word?

A more effective prayer life?

More knowledge of Jesus Christ?

An opportunity to win a neighbor to Christ?

When we find ourselves out in the desert, and new wilderness experiences await us, what does He promise?

"I will give waters in the wilderness, and rivers in the desert to give drink to my people, my chosen" (v. 20).

Spare the rod

*The rod of correction imparts wisdom, but a child
left to himself disgraces his mother. When the wicked
thrive, so does sin, but the righteous will see their
downfall. Discipline your son, and he will give
you peace; he will bring delight to your soul.*
Proverbs 29:15-17

$\mathcal{P}$ainful though it may be to spank that naughty but
darling child, still it is a commandment in the Bible to
parents. And both father and mother should stand
together in this important matter. The future of the
children depends upon it.

Discipline of the child, begun while he is very small,
is most effective when done in love. "Chasten thy son
while there is hope, and let not thy soul spare for his
crying (Pr 19:18). We are not to spank just for the sake
of spanking but we are admonished to give instruction
with the punishment.

"The rod *and reproof* give wisdom: but a child left to himself bringeth his mother to shame" (v. 15). Does this say also that mother should be sure she spends enough time with her child?

These are Bible orders which the conscientious Christian mother will carry out diligently, patiently, and prayerfully, being careful at the same time to set a good example. Then, we are promised, such consistent correction will be rewarded.

"Correct thy son, and he shall give thee rest; yea, he shall give delight to thy soul" (v. 17).

Who's who

*... I tell you the truth, no one can enter the kingdom
of God unless he is born of water and the Spirit ...
Just as Moses lifted up the snake in the desert, so
the Son of Man must be lifted up, that everyone
who believes in him may have eternal life ...
John 3:1-18*

Not many of us will find ourselves listed in *Who's
Who of American Women*. Biographies will be found
there of outstanding American women who have made
some contribution to the cultural or economic life of
our country. But God has His own *Who's Who*. The
Scriptures term it "The Book of Life." One need not
earn a doctor's degree, or even a bachelor's degree, to
be listed there. One does not have to be of any particular
race or color to be included, nor be rich or poor.

But there is one definite requirement which must be
met by all who would be named in this Book: "Ye must

be born again" (Jn 3:7).

Do you qualify?

Nicodemus possessed many qualifications, for he was "a master of Israel." But he lacked the one thing that would qualify him to have his name written in the Lamb's Book of Life. He had not been born again!

A ruler once came to Jesus by night,
To ask Him the way of salvation and light;
The Master made answer
in words true and plain,
"Ye must be born again."
~ W.T. Sleeper ~

Faith worketh patience

*... Consider it pure joy, my brothers, whenever
you face trials of many kinds, because you know
that the testing of your faith develops perseverance.
Perseverance must finish its work so that you may
be mature and complete, not lacking anything.*
James 1:1-4

Faith, work, and patience operate together. They are not to be separated. Believers are to exercise faith and then work and wait. If your faith goes to work, patience will follow. "That ye be not slothful, but followers of them who through faith and patience inherit the promises" (Heb 6:12).

In simple terms, faith works and patience waits. We see these three working together again in 1 Thessalonians 1:3 : "Remembering without ceasing your work of faith, and labor of love, and patience of hope in our Lord Jesus Christ."

Do you have these three spiritual friends in your life?

Someone has said, "Most footprints in the sands of time are made by workshoes."

Faith will either remove mountains or tunnel through.

My faith looks up to Thee,
Thou Lamb of Calvary,
Saviour divine!
Now hear me while I pray,
Take all my guilt away,
O let me from this day
Be wholly Thine!
~ Ray Palmer ~

That green-eyed monster

*But if you harbor bitter envy and selfish ambition
in your hearts, do not boast about it or deny the
truth. Such "wisdom" does not come down from
heaven but is earthly, unspiritual, of the devil ...*
James 3:14-18

*E*nvy will prevent us from getting the most out of life,
if we let it. Most of us would be happier if we could
lower our envy-jealousy quotient. We can make
ourselves miserable by grieving over the fact that Mrs.
Jones' clothes are so much smarter than ours.

So what? Accept it as a challenge and use it to see
how smart *you* can look on the amount of money you
have to spend. Make it a game and the results will
probably surprise even you.

Does a neighbor's new mink or expensive car bring to
the surface that green-eyed monster? Then stop and
count your own blessings! Maybe it took something like

this to make you see how much you really have to be thankful for.

A person who is fully aware of her own joys is not as likely to resent the joys of others. A sense of humor helps too. One who can laugh at her own shortcomings or misfortunes when her eyes start turning green, will undoubtedly be spared the pangs of envy.

There may always be someone who is richer, prettier, and smarter than you, but if the truth were known, that one probably envies you. You may have some talent that she doesn't possess.

There can be no peace of mind where "envying and strife is."

"And the fruit of righteousness is sown in peace of them that make peace" (v. 18).

The bread of wickedness

*Do not set foot on the path of the wicked or walk in
the way of evil men ... The path of the righteous is
like the first gleam of dawn shining ever brighter till the
full light of day. But the way of the wicked is like deep
darkness; they do not know what makes them stumble.*
Proverbs 4:14-19

It is not necessary to eat the "bread of wicked-ness" to
know how bitter it tastes. There are many dangers in
this kind of "bread". It is best not to investigate but to
pass by it altogether. We do not have to experiment with
certain things to know whether they are evil. It is
imperative that a child of God not allow himself to be
ensnared by the devil.

The way of wickedness is just the opposite from the
way of wisdom. We are advised to "enter not"; "go not
in"; "avoid it"; "turn from it". Travelers on the way of
wickedness have a food all their own. They eat the "bread

of wickedness" and drink the "wine of violence."

As a normal person partakes of food and drink, so do these wicked ones indulge in certain sins just as regularly. Sin becomes a definite part of their existence. Gradually this "food" becomes a part of them as food does for the normal body.

The believer's cup runs over with joy. His main source of energy is the "meat of the Word."

"Thy words were found, and I did eat them; and thy word was unto me the joy and rejoicing of mine heart" (Jer 15:16).

Turn on the light

*The path of the righteous is like the first gleam of dawn,
shining ever brighter till the full light of day. But the way of
the wicked is like deep darkness; they do not know what
makes them stumble. My son, pay attention to what I say ...
Proverbs 4:18-27*

$\mathcal{D}$id you ever stop at the close of a day to trace the guiding hand of God in your experiences of that day? Try it sometime!

One does not stand still in His Christian life. The closer one walks with Jesus the more light He will shed on the path. If we walk in the light on the path He chooses for us, we will find it "shineth more and more unto the perfect day." This light comes principally from His Word and this is why He tells us, "Attend to my words; incline thine ear unto my sayings."

We should never become careless about the Word of God. It should be used daily to guide our lives, then we will have the assurance that all our ways will be established. The way of light is the way of life. God's light will enable us to control lips, and eyes, and feet. We shall be led in a straight course unto the "perfect day." The light is there – turn it on!

Lead, kindly Light, amid th' encircling gloom,
Lead Thou me on:
The night is dark and I am far from home;
Lead Thou me on!
Keep Thou my feet; I do not ask to see
The distant scene; one step enough for me.
~ John H. Newman ~

Yesterday, today, and tomorrow

If that is how God clothes the grass of the field, which is here today and tomorrow is thrown into the fire, will he not much more clothe you, O you of little faith? ...
Matthew 6:30-34

Wouldn't you feel sorry for someone who never had burdens, trials, or tribulations? How could that one grow strong to meet the storms of life which inevitably come? Such a person might be likened to a marhsmallow – too soft and too sweet. How does an oak tree grow strong? Bending in the wind day by day, it develops resistance against the storms that beat upon it.

Yesterday is gone forever. I cannot undo any act of mine or unsay any word. All I can do at this point is commit all to God and pray for grace to do better tomorrow. I must be concerned with today. With faith in

God and trust in His promises I can fight the battles of today and bear its burdens.

"As thy days, so shall thy strength be" (Deu 33:25).

We are admonished to live but one day at a time and leave the yesterdays and tomorrows in the hands of the God of love. So let us journey but one day at a time.

"Day by day," the promise reads,
Daily strength for daily needs:
Cast foreboding fears away;
Take the manna of today.

Thou my daily task shalt give:
Day by day to thee I live;
So shall added years fulfill,
Not my own, my Father's will.
~ Josiah Conder ~

Endure hardness

*For this reason I remind you to fan into flame the
gift of God, which is in you through the laying on of
my hands. For God did not give us a spirit of timidity,
but a spirit of power, of love and of self-discipline ...*
2 Timothy 1:6-9

So long as we determine to faithfully serve our Lord
and bear witness to His saving grace, we may be sure
we will incur the wrath of Satan.

Should we let this discourage us? Not at all! Warfare
in a righteous cause can be most rewarding. "Fight the
good fight of faith, lay hold on eternal life" (1 Ti 6:12).
The way to get the most out of the Christian life is to
stand boldly for the truth.

Paul wrote to Timothy, "Thou therefore endure
hardness, as a good soldier of Jesus Christ" (2 Ti 2:3).
He is a poor soldier indeed who cannot "take it". With
the power of Christ working in us and through us, we

can withstand the attacks of our adversary, the devil, and do a real work for God.

> *Must I be carried to the skies*
> *On flowery beds of ease,*
> *While others fought to win the prize,*
> *And sailed through bloody seas?*
> *Sure I must fight if I would reign;*
> *Increase my courage, Lord;*
> *I'll bear the toil, endure the pain,*
> *Supported by thy word.*
> *~ Isaac Watts ~*

Delight in devotions

Give ear to my words, O Lord, consider my sighing. Listen
to my cry for help, my King and my God, for to you I pray.
In the morning, O Lord, you hear my voice; in the morning
I lay my requests before you and wait in expectation.
Psalm 5:1-3

*H*ow difficult it is in the early part of the day to sneak
away from the family, the telephone, and the household
duties, find a quiet place, and take in some food for the
soul!

Have there been days when there was not even time
for that piece of toast and cup of coffee in the early
morning, and as the day wore on you found yourself
becoming weak physically? Yet how foolish we are to
think that our spiritual life can be nourished and grow
strong without the necessary food for the soul, and that
on a day-by-day, meal-by-meal basis. One can lean all
day on a certain verse or passage of Scripture read during

the early morning hours.

Much can be learned from the practice of George Müller, the man of faith who lived in nineteenth century England. In reciting the pattern of his devotions he said, "The first thing to be concerned about was not how much I might serve the Lord; but how I might get my soul into a happy state, and how my inner man might be nourished."

Devotions at the outset of the day can be a real delight. Meditate on the Word of God and obtain food for the soul. The seeking soul will find there all that is needed; and the believing and obedient heart will be made happy in the Lord.

"O God, thou art my God; early will I seek thee" (Ps 63:1).

Advice and consent

*The wise woman builds her house, but with her
own hands the foolish one tears hers down ...
Proverbs 14:1-6*

"Mother, what should I do about – ?" "Mother, may I go to – ?" "Mother, is it all right if I– ?"

If there is one thing Mom has to do all day long, it is "advise and consent." A thousand and one decisions, small and great, must be made daily in every household. Because Dad is at work, this task usually falls to Mom.

The homemaker at the beginning of each day would do well to pray as did Moses, "So teach us to number our days, that we may apply our hearts unto wisdom" (Ps 90:12). The concerned mother will not absent-mindedly say yes or no to requests for permissions from her offspring. But she will carefully weigh the effects of that permission granted in the light of what is best for her child.

As for advice, the Christian mother finds the Bible a guide book for the rearing of her children "in the nurture and admonition of the Lord." Within its pages may be found wise instructions for parents and children.

"Wisdom is the principal thing; therefore get wisdom: and with all thy getting get under-standing" (Pr 4:7).

Daily bread

*This, then, is how you should pray: "Our Father
in heaven, hallowed be your name, your kingdom
come, your will be done on earth as it is in heaven.
Give us today our daily bread. Forgive us our debts,
as we also have forgiven our debtors. And lead us
not into temp-tation, but deliver us from the evil one."*
Matthew 6:9-13

$\mathcal{A}$t times, I have wished that I were a camel and
could take in a great quantity of nourishment at one time
and have it last for a long time. Like physical bread,
spiritual bread should be consumed at intervals.

In an effort to slim down some curves we put ourselves
on a rigid diet, yet we would not think of starving our
bodies. Often, though, we put ourselves on a spiritual
diet and starve our souls when we forget to take in our
daily supply of bread from God's Word.

It may be an old cliché but it is nevertheless true that

families that pray together stay together. God commanded the Israelites, "And these words, which I command thee this day, shall be in thine heart: and thou shalt teach them diligently unto thy children, and shalt talk of them when thou sittest in thine house, and when thou walkest by the way, and when thou liest down, and when thou risest up" (Deu 6:6,7).

We search the world for truth; we cull
The good, the pure, the beautiful,
From all old flower fields of the soul;
And, weary seekers of the best,
We come back laden from our quest,
To find that all the sages said
Is in the Book our mothers read.
~ John Greenleaf Whittier: Miriam ~

Entertain strangers

Then Jesus said to his host, "When you give a luncheon or dinner, do not invite your friends, your brothers or relatives, or your rich neighbors; if you do, they may invite you back and so you will be repaid. But when you give a banquet, invite the poor, the crippled, the lame, the blind, and you will be blessed. Although they cannot repay you, you will be repaid at the resurrection of the righteous."
Luke 14:12-14

*A*nything that is worthwhile takes work, and so does hospitality. There are so many things to think of – polishing the silver, setting the table, setting the house in order, scrubbing the children. But we are admonished to "Be not forgetful to entertain strangers." This does not mean that we are to go out into the highways and hedges and compel people we never laid eyes on to come in and have a cup of coffee! A time of relaxed social activity can help ease tensions as well as provide

90

opportunities to witness to unsaved neighbors and friends.

Coffee and apple pie do not require a great deal of work, yet they can be a hub around which good Christian fellowship revolves. We find in the Bible many examples of gracious entertainment in the home. While some thought they were entertaining a stranger, they were actually host to an angel.

Love should motivate us to open our hearts and homes and show others that we care. Many spiritual values are to be gained not only for ourselves, but also for our families and our guests. "Be not forgetful to entertain strangers: for thereby some have entertained angels unawares" (Heb 13:2).

The greatest of these is love

If I speak in the tongues of men and of angels, but
have not love, I am only a resounding gong ... And
now these three remain: faith, hope and love ...
1 Corinthians 13

We hear much in today's world about love. Most of
the songs about love sung by the modern rock groups
are not about the kind of love mentioned in this chapter
of God's Word. Most "love" em-phasis today is not
scriptural.

No love, it has been said, is as great as mother love.
Scriptural love of a mother for her child is the kind which
comforts when comfort is needed and chastens when
chastening is needed.

"Charity (love) beareth all things ... endureth all
things." This sometimes means the mother punishes her

child because she knows the child needs it, although it grieves her to have to do so, more than the punishment hurts the child. But she is comforted in her heart by the knowledge that her thoughts have been for the welfare and training of her child rather than for her own feelings.

What mother has not had to spank her child and then go off to her own room to cry after seeing her little one suffer under the chastening? She knows that for a time, at least, fellowship between them has been broken. So it must grieve the loving heart of God when He sees His children suffer for the sins they have brought upon themselves.

"He that loveth not knoweth not God; for God is love" (1 Jn 4:8).

God pardons like a mother
who kisses the offense
into everlasting forgetfulness.
~ Henry Ward Beecher ~

Things

*Then he called the crowd to him along with his disciples
and said: "If anyone would come after me, he must deny
himself and take up his cross and follow me ..."*
Mark 8:34-38

For some it is a collection of cups and saucers, each
with its particular story to tell. For others it is butterflies,
or guns, or stamps, or an Indian-head coin collection.
Things. Maybe it is an antique cupboard that belonged
to Grandmother, or the gold watch that was Uncle John's.
Things.

Nearly all of us have made a collection of something
or other. And there is no particular harm in such an
innocent hobby. But the danger comes in attaching too
much importance to these *things*. Perhaps we give too
much thought to them for "the morrow shall take thought
for the *things* of itself." "They that are after the flesh do
mind the things of the flesh; but they that are after the

Spirit the things of the Spirit" (Ro 8:5).

How much better it is to store up "things of the Spirit." For we are admonished to "Take heed, and beware of covetousness: for a man's life consisteth not in the abundance of the things which he possesseth" (Lk 12:15).

> *Take my silver and my gold,*
> *Not a mite would I withhold ...*
> *Take my moments and my days,*
> *Let them flow in endless praise.*
> *~ Frances R. Havergal ~*

Thoughts are things

Finally, brothers, whatever is true, whatever is noble, whatever is right, whatever is pure, whatever is lovely, whatever is admirable – if anything is excellent or praiseworthy – think about such things. Whatever you have learned or received or heard from me, or seen in me – put it into practice. And the God of peace will be with you.
Philippians 4:8-9

The thoughts one entertains are the things one enjoys, and what one enjoys reveals what one is. If we entertain only those thoughts that are true, honest, just, pure, lovely, of good report, there will be little time for us to think of things which are evil. In other words, if we fill our minds with pure thoughts we crowd out those that are impure.

The words "think" and "thank" come from the same root. One who "thinks" right will want to "thank," because as a man "thinketh in his heart, so is he." As we think about our blessings our hearts will overflow with thanksgiving. One who is thankful to another will be thoughtful of that one – it works two ways.

Now thank we all our God
With heart and hand and voices,
Who wondrous things hath done,
In whom His world rejoices;
Who, from our mother's arms,
Hath blessed us on our way
With countless gifts of love,
And still is ours today.
~ Martin Rinkart
Trans. by Catherine Winkworth ~

Thorn in the flesh

*But he said to me, "My grace is sufficient for you,
for my power is made perfect in weakness ..."*
2 Corinthians 12:9-11

"Why did this have to happen to me? What have I done to deserve this?"

There comes a time when we all ask these questions, feeling that a trial is undeserved and we are somehow being unjustly punished. These are times when God's promises scattered throughout His Word can be especially precious. His strength becomes greater in our weakness; His grace all-sufficient. When we turn it all over to Him, "the power of Christ" rests upon us.

Remembering that He knows the end from the beginning, our suffering is eased and the pain made bearable.

Paul was evidently tempted to believe that he could do a better work for His Lord if only that thorn in the

98

flesh could be removed. God knew, in His infinite wisdom, that Paul would be a better man with the thorn.

Trials would be easier to bear if we could remember that by enduring something which we may regard as a hindrance or a handicap, we can bring more glory to God than if that undesired thing was removed. The glorious fact is that these do not have to be borne in our own feeble strength, but by His power in us!

"My grace is sufficient for thee: for my strength is made perfect in weakness" (v. 9).

The mouth speaketh

... For by your words you will be acquitted,
and by your words you will be condemned.
Matthew 12:34-37

*H*ave you ever been seated in a restaurant next to a table of well-dressed men and found that their conversation, clearly audible at your table, was constantly punctuated with profanity? These same individuals would not dream of coughing in your face or sneezing into your food, yet they freely use foul language within your hearing range. Why do they do it?

Is it a mark of manliness? Does it indicate how clearly one's mind operates; or does it make his conversation more pleasing? One thing is clear – it is offensive to those of good breeding and Christian principle, and it is dishonoring to God who said. "Thou shalt not take the name of the Lord thy God in vain."

A famous writer tells us that in no other civilized nation

is blasphemy part and parcel of the everyday speech of men, women, and even children, as it is in America. Profanity is a foul habit that degrades the user and dishonors a holy God. Let us teach our children to help eliminate this plague from our society.

"I will take heed to my ways, that I sin not with my tongue: I will keep my mouth with a bridle, while the wicked is before me" (Ps 39:1).

Take my lips and let them be
Filled with messages from Thee.
~ Frances R. Havergal ~

The bread of affliction

*Do not eat it with bread made with yeast, but for seven days
eat unleavened bread, the bread of affliction, because you
left Egypt in haste – so that all the days of your life you may
remember the time of your departure from Egypt.*
Deuteronomy 16:3

*... and say, "This is what the king says: Put
this fellow in prison and give him nothing
but bread and water until I return safely."*
2 Chronicles 18:26

There are few of us who have not at one time or another
eaten "the bread of affliction." Mature in Christ though
we may be, in our humanity and weakness some of the
afflictions our loving Lord sends into our lives are hard
to bear. Does this mean God does not love us or has
turned His back on us? On the contrary, "Whom the Lord
loveth He chasteneth." Because the mother punishes her

child for wrongdoing means she does love that child.

So God would be unjust to His children if He did not bring us back onto the straight path when we had strayed into sin. Many Christians will testify that God's chastening brought them into closer fellowship with Him, and when it was all over, they praised Him for sending it. Have you ever thanked God for your afflictions? Certainly this goes against the grain. But are we wholly consecrated to Him if we rebel against what He sends?

"Who shall separate us from the love of Christ? Shall tribulation, or distress, or persecution, or famine, or nakedness, or peril, or sword? As it is written, For thy sake we are killed all the day long; we are accounted as sheep for the slaughter. Nay, in all these things we are more than conquerors through him that loved us" (Ro 8:35-37).

Obedience

... To obey is better than sacrifice, and to heed is better than the fat of rams. For rebellion is like the sin of divination, and arrogance like the evil of idolatry. Because you have rejected the word of the Lord, he has rejected you as king.
1 Samuel 15:21-23

What mother's heart is not warmed when her child timidly approaches, holding out an awkwardly wrapped gift, purchased with a few pennies saved from an allowance. The act speaks words that the child is not able to utter, and the mother's heart responds in love. But dearer to the mother's heart than this beautiful gesture is an obedient child, one who shows his love by obedience for "to obey is better than sacrifice, and to hearken than the fat of rams."

An outward effort to obedience is not enough; a child must obey in his heart if he is to please his mother. So must God's child obey in his heart as well as in his

104

actions, if he is to please God.

The Lord Jesus set the standard of heart attitude above mere outward practice for He declared, "This people draweth nigh unto me with their mouth, and honoureth me with their lips; but their heart is far from me" (Mt 15:8).

This, then, must be the case. The desire in the heart to obey should prompt the outward act of obedience. The child who loves his mother in his heart has little difficulty in obeying her.

In this day of grace, the commandments must still be kept in the heart, and there must be love and esteem if the commandments are to be obeyed.

We'll bring the little duties
We have to do each day;
We'll try our best to please Him,
At home, at school, at play:
And better are these treasures
To offer to our King,
Than richest gifts without them;
Yet these a child may bring.
~ The Book of Praise for Children, 1881 ~

Peace

If you follow my decrees and are careful to
obey my commands, I will send you rain in
its season, and the ground will yield its crops
and the trees of the field their fruit ...
Leviticus 26:3-7

In the symbols painted on walls or worn on necklaces, in the voices of young people carrying picket signs, we receive one main message these days: peace now. It is rather strange to notice that often those who demonstrate so loudly for peace, end up using violence themselves. "They speak not peace: but they devise deceitful matters against them that are quiet in the land" (Ps 35:20). There is a peace, however, that is available to all for the asking – peace with God through our Lord Jesus Christ. This peace cannot be found at any peace table, summit meeting, by winning a war, or signing a treaty.

The world gives peace as a doctor gives an anesthetic;

Christ gives peace that is life, and hope, and strength. Christ gives heart peace. The peace of the world operates only in favorable circumstances. The peace of Christ is effectual in any circumstance.

By confident reliance upon the Lord, the believer may enjoy the peace of God in the midst of the alarming and disturbing circumstances of life. A heart and mind at rest amid the storms of life, guarded by the peace of God – this is real peace.

"Peace I leave with you, my peace I give unto you: not as the world giveth, give I unto you" (Jn 14:27).

Happy New Year

But the land you are crossing the Jordan to take posses-
sion of is a land of mountains and valleys that drinks
rain from heaven. It is a land the Lord your God
cares for; the eyes of the Lord your God are continu-
ally on it from the beginning of the year to its end.
Deuteronomy 11:11-12

On January 1, we stand upon the verge of an unknown year. There lie before us 365 new days, and we should march toward them with confidence. None can tell what we shall encounter, what changes will come, or what new experiences await. The housewife delights in crisp new curtains for her clean windows; a fresh coat of paint on a soiled wall; a new piece of furniture in a vacant spot. Housekeeping chores take on a new dimension and seem to lose some of their drudgery.

But there are other areas in our lives where many of us would like to have a fresh start. L.F. Tarkington has written a poem called, *The Land of Beginning Again*, which comes to mind at the beginning of each new year. We would all like to take a trip to that magic land, and we do every New Year.

Backed by God's Word, we have the comforting and cheering message that if we commit our days to Him one by one, He will be with us "from the beginning of the year even unto the end of the year" (v. 12).

Behold, another year begins!
Set out afresh for heaven;
Seek pardon for thy former sins,
In Christ so freely given.
Devoutly yield thyself to God,
And on His grace depend;
With zeal pursue the heavenly road,
Nor doubt a happy end.
~ Simon Browne ~

Are you lonely?

No one will be able to stand up against you all the days of your life. As I was with Moses, so I will be with you; I will never leave you nor forsake you ...
Joshua 1:5-9

Do you feel that your life's work is done now that you have reared your children and they have gone from home? Do the hours of your day seem endless? Loneliness has led many an otherwise healthy person to the doctor's office or to the psychiatrist's couch. And older people are not the only lonely people in the world. Many children are lonely because their parents have too little time for them. Teenagers are often lonely because they feel misunderstood. Some married couples are lonely because they feel misunderstood. Some married couples are lonely because work separates them.

It should be comforting to know that there are times when we need to be alone, to strengthen our inner stability and restore serenity for busier days. The psalmist tells us, "He leadeth me beside the still waters. He restoreth my soul" (Ps 23:2-3).

Why not put to good use these free hours (which you never had before) in service for the Lord? Surely there are many less fortunate souls who would be cheered by a visit, a newsy letter, or a friendly telephone call.

It was alone the Saviour
prayed in dark Gethsemane;
Alone He drained the bitter
cup and suffered there for me.
~ Ben H. Price ~

Mother as teacher

... When Jesus landed and saw a large crowd, he had compassion on them, because they were like sheep without a shepherd. So he began teaching them many things.
Mark 6:32-34

To her children, mother has to be a doctor, lawyer, teacher, preacher. One of the greatest privileges she has though is to be able to teach them certain Christian principles which can only be learned in the home. Her personal faith, peerless manners, and subtle wisdom in her relationships with others, is the birthright of her children.

Jesus as the perfect teacher possessed more qualifications of a good teacher than just a thorough knowledge of the subject matter. He was "moved with compassion," which is a necessary ingredient for becoming a good teacher. A love for the one being taught is essential in good teaching.

No one was ever more patient nor as kind as the Saviour. If Mother's teaching is to be effective she must cultivate these characteristics of the Saviour.

An angel paused in his downward flight
With a seed of truth and love and light;
And he said, "Where must this seed be sown
To bring most fruit when it is grown?"
The Master heard what he said and smiled,
"Go plant it for Me in the heart of a child."
~ Selected ~

His seed begging bread

*... For the Lord loves the just and will not forsake
his faithful ones. They will be protected forever,
but the offspring of the wicked will be cut off.*
Psalm 37:18-28

*G*od does not forsake His people. Not only does David
say, I have "not seen the righteous forsaken, nor his seed
begging bread" (v. 25), but this is reiterated in verse 28:
"The Lord ... forsaketh not His saints."

God's way is to reward righteousness and to punish
sin. "Say ye to the righteous, that it shall be well with
him ... Woe unto the wicked! it shall be ill with him" (Is
3:10-11). Our only possibility of righteousness is through
Christ.

The child of God is "His seed" but one who begs bread
is someone who is in abject need with no resource. The
two pictures do not fit together because the child of God,
through Christ, has available to him all the resources of

his heavenly Father.

Many troubled hearts have leaned upon His promise, "I will never leave thee, nor forsake thee" (Heb 13:5).

My Father is rich in houses and lands,
He holdeth the wealth of the world in His hands!
Of rubies and diamonds, of silver and gold,
His coffers are full; He has riches untold.
I'm the child of a King, the child of a King!
With Jesus, my Saviour, I'm the child of a King!
~ Hattie E. Buell ~

With thanksgiving

Come, let us sing for joy to the Lord; let us
shout aloud for the Rock of our salvation ...
Psalm 95

The foundation of all prayer should be laid with thanksgiving. God desires that we be mindful of present blessings and past petitions granted, when we come before Him invoking divine favor. It could be that before we begin the asking, our loving God would have us stop and count our present blessings.

Every day ought to be a Thanksgiving Day for the child of God. Strange it is that we do not ordinarily recognize the common mercies of life. We have to see a blind man led by his dog, before we realize what a wonderful thing it is to be able to see. We have to see one who is lame before we are thankful for two good feet. A shame it is that we are so dull it takes the misfortunes of others to rouse us to acknowledge our own blessings.

"Who can tell how much a bird means by its song? The aroma of the flowers smells like incense, and the mist arising from the river looks like the smoke of a morning sacrifice. Oh, that we were as responsive!" said T. DeWitt Talmage.

How often do we thank God for the cool, sweet water we drink; the pure fresh air we breathe; the ability to hear someone say, "I love you?"

"O give thanks unto the Lord; for he is good: for his mercy endureth for ever" (Ps 106:1).

Thine own understanding

My son, do not forget my teaching, but keep my commands in your heart, for they will prolong your life many years and bring you prosperity ...
Proverbs 3:1-6

To lean upon one's own understanding is to trust a frail and insecure support. This is to form and execute one's own plans in an independent spirit of self-confidence and self-reliance. Now these qualities can be good, when supported by the power of God. When we proceed without Him, we are living as if there were no God. One does not need a God if he can work out his own destiny. What folly!

As a child leans upon the wisdom, strength, and care of his parents, to trust in the Lord is to put full confidence in Him – to fully rely upon Him. This means one's entire commitment to the grace and truth of God with the abandonment of every attempt to save oneself by one's

118

own strength or wisdom. God waits to care for, provide for, and sustain His own. The secret is to submit your will to His holy will. Then "He shall direct thy path."

Knowing all things, He knows what is best for His own and leads wisely and safely.

God never deceives; but man is deceived whenever he puts too much trust in himself. Man proposes, but God disposes.
~ Thomas A Kempis ~

A good name

*... He spoke to them from the pillar of cloud; they
kept his statutes and the decrees he gave them ...
Psalm 99*

Most of us go to great lengths to protect our good
name. The wise Solomon said, "A good name is rather
to be chosen than great riches" (Pr 22:1). We who know
Him bear the name of the Lord Jesus. The impression
unsaved men have of our Saviour and His salvation, is
made from what they see in our lives. "Ye are our epistle
written in our hearts, known and read of all men: ...
written not with ink, but with the Spirit of the living
God; not in tables of stone, but in fleshy tables of the
heart" (2 Co 3:2-3).

James writes in his epistle that the ungodly rich
"blaspheme that worthy name by the which ye are called"
(Ja 2:7) referring to that beautiful name of our Lord Jesus
Christ; the name "which is above every name," the name

in which alone we have salvation.

"Neither is there salvation in any other: for there is none other name under heaven given among men, whereby we must be saved" (Acts 4:12). Let us bear His name worthily!

The name of Jesus is so sweet,
I love its music to repeat;
It makes my joys full and complete,
The precious name of Jesus.
I love the name of Him whose heart
Knows all my griefs, and bears a part;
Who bids all anxious fears depart –
I love the name of Jesus.
~ W.C. Martin ~

The quiet time

Do you not know? Have you not heard? The Lord
is the everlasting God, the Creator of the ends
of the earth. He will not grow tired or weary,
and his understanding no one can fathom ...
Isaiah 40:28-31

Who more than today's busy mother needs to "run,
and not be weary," to "walk and not faint"? For the
Christian wife and mother this is essential. Prayer and
the reading of God's Word are her lifeline to strength
and wisdom for the untrodden path of the hours ahead.
In this way she can have the assurance of His presence
by her side and feel strengthened spiritually to meet the
problems of the day.

Something will have to give if opportunity is to be
found for this quiet time with God. Nothing should be
allowed to interfere with it. There will be days when
you will have to fight to preserve it. But what is any

more important? The entire family will benefit from your inner strength and you can impart to them something from the loving source. Can you remember a day, however smooth the sailing, when you did not need a measure of strength, courage, wisdom, and guidance? You will find it right there in God's Word!

"Open thou mine eyes, that I may behold wondrous things out of thy law" (Ps 119:18).

Thou callest me to seek Thy face,
'Tis all I wish to seek;
To attend the whispers of Thy grace,
And hear Thee only speak.
With Thee conversing, we forget
All time, and toil, and care;
Labor is rest, and pain is sweet,
If Thou, my God, art here.
~ Charles Wesley ~

A lift for your life

*Give ear to my words, O Lord, consider
my sighing. Listen to my cry for help, my
King and my God, for to you I pray ...*
Psalm 5:1-3

We would be wise to begin the day with a prayer to God. It will sweeten and gladden us from the start. We are exhorted to "die daily," and it is best to die to self and sin early each morning.

Direct a prayer to God, a prayer of thanks for the rest of another night and the light of another day; a prayer of thanks for the opportunities and privileges, the joys and the blessings that come with each new day; a prayer of supplication asking for strength to meet and fulfill the responsibilities that press so heavily upon every child of God.

Ask for wisdom to solve the many problems that crowd into every day. Ask for power and perception to deal with others, and for a filling of the Holy Spirit in order to do His will. Pray and look up. Look up for the smile of His approval. Behold His handiwork in the heavens, and listen for His voice. Look up and be assured that God is there. "In the morning will I direct my prayer unto thee, and will look up" (v, 3).

"I will lift up mine eyes unto the hills, from whence cometh my help. My help cometh from the Lord, which made heaven and earth" (Ps 121:1-2).

The bread of adversity

*... Although the Lord gives you the bread of adversity
and the water of affliction, your teachers will be hidden
no more; with your own eyes you will see them ...*
Isaiah 30:18-21

Someone has said, "It is not what happens to you, but
the way you take it that counts." Can you "take it"? Life
can be managed when all goes well, but what do we do
when adversity strikes? Then and only then do we show
our true colors. How easy it is to think that every other
person's burden is light while our own is heavy. Too
often it is our fancy rather than our fate.

When the "bread of adversity" must be eaten, it does
only harm to "kick against the pricks" and hurt the feet.
As a tree bows in the wind, so must we in the face of
adversity. Grumbling is a bad habit for the child of God,
and when we complain we miss a blessing. The rainbow
will follow the rain as surely as God is on His throne.

Every night breaks into morning.

> *Let sorrow do its work,*
> *Send grief or pain;*
> *Sweet are Thy messengers,*
> *Sweet their refrain,*
> *When they can sing with me,*
> *More love, O Christ, to Thee,*
> *More love to Thee!*
> *~ Elizabeth P. Prentiss ~*